W9-CLS-362

PRESIDENTS *and* FIRST LADIES

Bill & Hillary Rodham
Clinton

By

Ruth Ashby

WORLD ALMANAC® LIBRARY

Please visit our web site at: www.worldalmanaclibrary.com
For a free color catalog describing World Almanac® Library's list of high-quality books
and multimedia programs, call 1-800-848-2928 (USA) or 1-800-387-3178 (Canada).
World Almanac® Library's fax: (414) 332-3567.

Library of Congress Cataloging-in-Publication Data

Ashby, Ruth.
    Bill & Hillary Rodham Clinton / by Ruth Ashby.
      p. cm — (Presidents and first ladies)
    Includes bibliographical references and index.
    ISBN 0-8368-5756-9 (lib. bdg.)
    ISBN 0-8368-5762-3 (softcover)
    1. Clinton, Bill, 1946-—Juvenile literature. 2. Presidents—United States—Biography—Juvenile
literature. 3. Clinton, Hillary Rodham—Juvenile literature. 4. Presidents' spouses—United States—
Biography—Juvenile literature. 5. Married people—United States—Biography—Juvenile literature.
I. Title: Bill and Hillary Rodham Clinton. II. Title.
  E886.A83   2005
  973.929'092'2—dc22
  [B]   2004059642

First published in 2005 by
World Almanac® Library
330 West Olive Street, Suite 100
Milwaukee, WI 53132 USA

Copyright © 2005 by Byron Preiss Visual Publications, Inc.

Produced by Byron Preiss Visual Publications, Inc.
Project Editor: Kelly Smith
Photo Researcher: Larry Schwartz
Designed by Four Lakes Colorgraphics Inc.
World Almanac® Library editorial direction: Mark J. Sachner
World Almanac® Library editor: Jenette Donovan Guntly
World Almanac® Library art direction: Tammy West
World Almanac® Library graphic designer: Melissa Valuch
World Almanac® Library production: Jessica Morris

Photo Credits:
AP/Wide World Photos: 11, 12, 20, 21, 22 (top and bottom), 23, 24, 26, 28 (top and bottom), 30, 31,
32 (top and bottom), 33, 36 (top and bottom), 37, 38, 39, 40, 42; Clinton Presidential Library: 5,
6 (bottom), 7, 14, 16, 17 (top and bottom); CORBIS: 6 (top), 8, 10, 15, 19, 41; Nancy Kaszerman/
ZUMA Press: 4 (bottom); The White House: 4 (top)
Cover art: CORBIS (right); The White House (left)

Printed in Canada

1 2 3 4 5 6 7 8 9 09 08 07 06 05

CONTENTS

Words that appear in the glossary are printed in
boldface type the first time they occur in the text.

★ INTRODUCTION ★ ★ ★ ★ ★ ★ ★ ★ ★

On November 7, 2000, Bill and Hillary Clinton and their daughter, Chelsea, went to the polling place in their new hometown of Chappaqua, New York, for a very special occasion. For the first time in the Clintons' twenty-five-year marriage, Hillary's name was on the ballot instead of Bill's. "Chelsea and I voted first," Bill recalled later, "then hugged each other as we watched Hillary close the curtain and cast a ballot for herself"—for senator from New York.

William Jefferson Clinton, forty-second president of the United States.

It was the latest breathtaking curve in a roller-coaster relationship that had taken the brilliant, ambitious duo from the ivy-covered halls of Yale Law School to the halls of power in Washington, D.C. One of the most controversial First Couples in history, the Clintons had presided over a decade marked by prosperity and wracked by scandal. Less than two years before the 2000 election, Bill Clinton had become only the second president in U.S. history to be **impeached**, the result of an illicit relationship with a White House intern that forever tainted his presidency and nearly ended his marriage. Yet, despite everything, Bill and Hillary have stayed together.

Hillary has her own explanation of why she and Bill remained married. "All I know is that no one understands me better and no one can make me laugh the way Bill does," she wrote in her autobiography, *Living History*. "Even after all these years, he is still the most interesting, energizing, and fully alive person I have ever met. Bill Clinton and I started a conversation in the spring of 1971, and more than thirty years later we're still talking."

First Lady Hillary Rodham Clinton.

★ ★

CHAPTER ONE

THE BOY FROM HOPE

On the hot night of August 19, 1946, William Jefferson Blythe III was born in a hospital in the little town of Hope, Arkansas. His father was not present. Three months earlier, the car that Bill Blythe was driving through a dark, rainy night had run off the road, and Blythe was thrown from the car. He drowned in a drainage ditch in a few feet of water. The newborn baby would be raised by his mother, Virginia Cassidy Blythe, a registered nurse. Never knowing his father, Bill Clinton said later, left him with the feeling that he had to "live for two people. . . . Even when I wasn't sure where I was going, I was always in a hurry."

Soon Virginia decided to go back to school to get her degree as a nurse anesthetist. She left Billy in the care of her parents, Edith and James Eldridge Cassidy. His grandmother, Clinton recalled, wanted him to "eat a lot, learn a lot, and always be neat and clean. [She] would sit me up in the high chair at breakfast and tack playing cards on the baseboards to the windows and make me count, and teach me to read, and add, and subtract." He spent hours in his grandfather's grocery store, raiding the cookie jar and playing with the local children, many of whom were African American. Arkansas was a segregated state in the 1950s, but Eldridge Cassidy made it a point to treat his white customers and black customers equally. Bill didn't realize, he said later, that he was the only white boy in all of Hope who was allowed to play with black kids.

Billy Blythe in Hope, Arkansas, in 1950. Young Billy was a happy little boy, much loved and even a bit spoiled by his doting grandparents.

Bill's first childhood home, in Hope, Arkansas. This was his grandparent's home, where he and his mother lived until she married a car salesman named Roger Clinton.

Setting Goals

When Billy was four, his mother married a car salesman named Roger Clinton. Three years later, they moved to Hot Springs, Arkansas, an old resort and gambling town. By then Billy was a chunky, curly-haired, very friendly boy with a big smile and an interest in everything. It didn't take his teachers long to discover that he was one of the smartest students they had ever seen. He got A's in every subject—except good behavior. Billy was so bright, the teachers told Virginia, that he wouldn't give the other children the chance to contribute. In short, he talked too much.

Billy had a busy, active childhood—he read nearly all the books in the local library, worshiped in the local Baptist church, and played tenor saxophone in the school band. When he was

Bill, his mother Virginia, and his half-brother Roger in the summer of 1959, when Bill turned thirteen.

ten, he got his first taste of politics by watching the August 1956 Democratic and Republican National Conventions on television. He was fascinated. On July 25, 1956, he was thrilled to welcome a new baby brother named Roger Jr. Often he helped his mother out by baby-sitting Roger when she went to work.

All was not well at home, however. Roger Clinton Sr. had a bad drinking problem, and when he drank, he sometimes became angry and abusive. When Billy was just five, his stepfather fired a gun into the wall of their home and was thrown in jail. Later Clinton admitted that he had to "learn to live with the darker side of life at a fairly early period." Increasingly, Virginia Clinton found herself relying on her older son to protect both her and little Roger, who was terrified of his father. Matters came to a head one night in 1960, when Roger came home in a drunken rage and started to beat Bill's mother. Fourteen and already taller than his stepfather, Bill broke down the bedroom door. "Daddy, I want you on your feet," he demanded.

Roger Clinton pulled himself up. "Hear me," Bill said, looking straight into his eyes. "Don't you ever touch my mother again."

Roger made an effort to reform but soon relapsed. In April 1962, Virginia finally moved herself and the two boys out of the house and filed for divorce. At the same time, young Bill Blythe went to the county clerk's office and filed for a name change—to William Jefferson Clinton. Later he explained that he wanted the same last name as his stepbrother, Roger. After Roger Sr. promised once again to mend his ways, Virginia took him back. However, from then until the day he died in 1967, Roger Clinton remained an alcoholic, a sad and bitter figure.

The highlight of Bill Clinton's high school career was being chosen as one of two Arkansas representatives to Boys Nation, a program that brought promising young men to the nation's capital and introduced them to the business of politics. During one unforgettable week in the summer of 1963, Bill lunched in the **Senate** dining room with Arkansas senator J. William Fulbright and went to the Rose Garden at the White House to meet President John F. Kennedy. Determined to greet the president face to face, Bill pressed to the front of the student group and shook Kennedy's hand. "When he came back from Washington, holding this picture of himself with Jack Kennedy," his mother recalled, "and the expression on his face . . . I knew right then that politics was the answer for him."

Sixteen-year-old Bill Clinton shakes hands with President John F. Kennedy in the Rose Garden at the White House, July 26, 1963. Bill would remember this inspiring moment for the rest of his life.

A Brilliant Student

Bill wanted to go back to Washington so badly that he applied to only one college: Georgetown University's School of Foreign Service, where he would major in international government studies. Within two months after his arrival, the brash, self-confident Arkansan had become president of the freshman class. In the summer, he worked in a local governor's race, and in his junior year, he got two part-time jobs in Senator Fulbright's office. At the end of his four years, he applied for a prestigious Rhodes scholarship to study at Oxford University in England. When he was accepted, he phoned Virginia to tell her the good news. "Well, mother, how do you think I'll look in English tweed?" he asked.

In fall 1968, the 6-foot-3-inch (191-centimeter) tall twenty-two-year-old sailed to England on the USS *United States* with other

international students. When Clinton arrived at Oxford, a fellow student recalled, "He greeted every reluctant, shy, perfectly mannered English schoolboy with a big grin, a hearty handshake, and a serious dose of down-home Americana. Some of them have never recovered." One of his best friends at Oxford was future author and diplomat Strobe Talbott. "He was quite outstanding, even as a young man," Talbott remembered, "for the way in which he combined a very obvious and eloquent idealism . . . with a practical sense of politics."

Bill Clinton (center) poses with other Rhodes scholars at Oxford University in the fall of 1968. A year later, like many of his generation, the clean-cut student grew long hair and a beard.

Difficult Decisions

The biggest international issue at Oxford was the ongoing Vietnam War. Clinton, like most of the rest of his friends, felt that the war was unjust, yet he was in danger of being **drafted**. He knew that whatever his beliefs, his political future would be doomed if he simply refused to serve and became a "draft resister." Instead, the brilliant student wrangled a **deferment** in 1968 by agreeing to attend the University of Arkansas (UA) Law School for his sophomore year and join the Reserved Officers Training Corps (ROTC).

He had been saved from the draft—but then had second thoughts. He didn't really want to go to UA Law School. After spending the summer at home, he went back to England and attended Oxford in 1969. That December, draftees were chosen by lottery, in which a person was assigned a number based on his birthday. Clinton's lottery number was 311 out of a possible 365. It was so high he knew he would never be called into service.

Bill felt free to write a letter to the head of the ROTC program, Colonel Eugene Holmes, explaining his dilemma and his choice. He had decided not to become a draft resister, Clinton explained, so that he could maintain his "political viability within the system." But he was against the draft and against his country's involvement in Vietnam. "No government rooted in limited, parliamentary democracy should have the power to make its citizens fight and kill and die in a war they may oppose," Clinton wrote, "a war which even possibly may be wrong. . . . " It was a letter that would come back to haunt him.

The following fall, Clinton received a scholarship to Yale Law School in New Haven, Connecticut. In his second semester, he spotted a woman in his political and civil rights class whom he hadn't seen before. "She had thick dark blond hair and wore eyeglasses and no makeup," he remembered, "but she conveyed a sense of strength and self-possession that I had rarely seen in anyone, man or woman." He decided he had to meet her.

The Vietnam War

By 1969, the year Bill Clinton was almost drafted, the war in Vietnam had already dragged on for more than ten years. Vietnam had been divided into two nations in 1954—**Communist** North Vietnam, supported by the Soviet Union, and South Vietnam, supported by the United States. When a civil war broke out, then-president Dwight D. Eisenhower sent military advisors to help the South Vietnamese. He was convinced that if all of Vietnam became Communist, the rest of Southeast Asia would fall to Communism, too, like a row of dominoes. Later, President John F. Kennedy increased U.S. involvement, and President Lyndon B. Johnson escalated it sharply. By spring 1968, about 414 young American men were being killed and 1,160 men were being wounded in Vietnam each week.

Increasingly, Americans were questioning the war's high cost in terms of human life. Antiwar protesters marched, wrote, and burned **draft cards**. Young men eligible for the draft faced a difficult choice: to serve, to resist, or to find a safe alternative such as the National Guard, the ROTC, or a student deferment. In his 2004 autobiography, *My Life*, Bill Clinton summed up the decisions his generation made: "During the Vietnam era, 16 million men avoided military service through legal means; 8.7 enlisted; 2.2 million were drafted; only 209,000 were alleged to have dodged the draft or resisted, of whom 8,750 were convicted."

By the time a cease-fire was declared in 1973, about fifty-seven thousand American soldiers had died in action. Two years after the United States withdrew, North Vietnam overran South Vietnam.

STAR STUDENT

Hillary Diane Rodham was born in Chicago on October 26, 1947, the first child of Hugh and Dorothy Howell Rodham. Three years later, the family moved to suburban Park Ridge, Illinois, a **conservative** middle-class town with wide, tree-lined streets, safe neighborhoods, and good public schools. Her father commuted every day to Chicago, where he owned a drapery business. Her mother was a homemaker whose life revolved around Hillary and her two younger brothers, Hugh Jr. and Tony.

When Hillary started kindergarten, her mother told her that school would be a "great adventure . . . she was going to learn great things, live new passions." Dorothy Rodham wanted her daughter to be strong and self-confident. Once, soon after the family moved to Park Ridge, Hillary came to her mother crying that another little girl was hitting her.

The Rodhams' comfortable two-story brick home in Park Ridge, Illinois, where Hillary grew up.

"Go back out there," Dorothy Rodham told her, "and if Suzy hits you, you have my permission to hit her back. You have to stand up for yourself. There's no room in this house for cowards."

Hillary did as her mother said and reported back later. "I can play with the boys now," she said excitedly, "and Suzy will be my friend!"

Hillary's father, Hugh Sr., had learned the value of hard work and thrift while growing up in the factory town of Scranton, Pennsylvania. Often gruff and uncommunicative, he rarely praised his children, once telling Hillary when she came home with a straight-A report card that she "must go to a pretty easy school." Yet he was generous with his time, tutoring her in math before school and practicing softball with her in the evenings.

Lessons in Leadership

Owing in large part to her parents' influence, Hillary became an assertive leader. She was always a dedicated student who loved to read and enjoyed participating in classroom debates. A fairly good athlete, she especially enjoyed ice skating, summer league softball, and swimming. Although her high school was huge, with five thousand students, Hillary managed to emerge early on as a student leader, becoming a student council representative. In her junior year, she served as class vice president.

Hillary Rodham in her 1965 high school graduation photo.

When Hillary was fourteen, a new youth minister, Reverend Don Jones, joined Hillary's church, the First United Methodist Church of Park Ridge. Jones believed that Christianity was "faith in action." During Thursday night classes he called the "University of Life," students talked about religion and civil rights and other social issues. With other members of her youth group, Hillary came into contact with people outside her suburban community. They met with gang members in inner-city Chicago neighborhoods and baby-sat for the children of farmworkers in rural **migrant camps**. One Sunday in 1962, Jones took his students to Orchestra Hall in Chicago to hear Dr. Martin Luther King Jr. give a speech. Afterward, Hillary was thrilled to go backstage and shake the great man's hand.

As a girl, Hillary was a conservative Republican like her father (her mother was secretly a Democrat). During the 1964 presidential election between Republican Barry Goldwater and Democrat Lyndon B. Johnson, Hillary worked for the Goldwater campaign and wore a sash that said "Goldwater Girl."

A Time of Change

Hillary's politics began to alter after high school when she went east to Wellesley College in Massachusetts. There, she and her dormmates spent hours discussing politics and ideas. As the Vietnam War raged, she realized that, like many Americans, she felt the war was a mistake. She helped organize a series of long meetings on campus, called teach-ins, about the Vietnam War.

Hillary was appalled by the assassination of Dr. Martin Luther King Jr. on April 4, 1968. Hillary stormed into her dorm room, her roommate remembered, "the door flew back, and her book bag went crashing against the wall. She was completely distraught by the horror of it." Together with thousands of other students, Hillary put on a black armband and went to Boston to mourn King's death.

That summer, Hillary seized the opportunity to go to Washington, D.C., on the Wellesley Internship Program. For nine weeks, she worked for **House Minority Leader** Gerald Ford and other **moderate** Republicans and attended the Republican Convention in Miami. Later that summer, back in Park Ridge, she and a friend sneaked off to the Democratic Convention in Chicago. She was shocked to see Vietnam protesters riot outside the convention center and the police attack the crowd with tear gas and nightsticks.

Hillary returned to Wellesley that fall and was elected president of the student government. In May 1969, she became the first Wellesley student ever to speak at graduation. She spoke immediately after Senator Edward Brooke, a moderate Republican. After his extremely mild speech, Hillary scolded Brooke for offering nothing but "sympathy" to young people who were disillusioned by their government and searching for a way to make their own mark on the world. "We've had lots of sympathy," she told him, "but

Women demonstrate for equal rights in front of the Statue of Liberty on August 10, 1970.

we feel that for too long our leaders have used politics as the art of the possible. And the challenge now is to practice making what appears to be impossible, possible."

Some of the faculty and parents in the audience felt that Hillary was being rude, but her fellow students loved what she said. A month later, she was featured in *Life* magazine as one of the nation's new young leaders.

After a summer working in a fish processing plant in Alaska, Hillary went to Yale Law School, one of just twenty-seven women in a class of 235. Hillary Rodham, already a star, served on the Board of Editors of the prestigious law journal *Yale Review of Law and Social Action*. One day, in the student lounge, she heard a big student with a beard and mop of brown hair boast, "And not only that, we grow the biggest watermelons in the world."

"Who is that?" she asked a friend.

"Oh, that's Bill Clinton. He's from Arkansas."

Women's Liberation

After nearly seventy-five years of struggle, women in the United States finally won the right to vote in 1920. True political and social equality, however, remained a distant dream. Women were paid much less than men for doing the same work, and many professions were closed to women altogether.

In the 1960s, the women's liberation movement fought for equality in the workplace and in the home. Feminist Betty Friedan founded the National Organization for Women (NOW) in 1966 "to bring American women into full participation in the mainstream of American society."

By 1970, previously all-male schools such as Harvard and Yale had opened their doors to women, who were also entering law, medical, and business schools in large numbers for the first time. In addition, the introduction of the birth control pill in 1960 gave women new control over their bodies and choices about family planning.

The changing roles of men and women and the new sexual freedom created a backlash among some conservative Americans. Modern, ambitious young women like Hillary Rodham Clinton were caught in the crossfire between the old ways and the new.

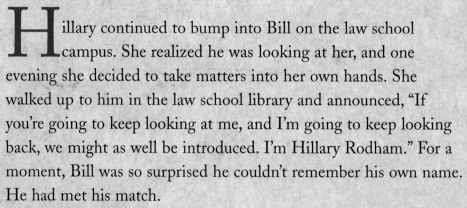

CHAPTER THREE

TWO FOR THE PRICE OF ONE

Bill Clinton and Hillary Rodham, young and in love, at Yale Law School in New Haven, Connecticut.

Hillary continued to bump into Bill on the law school campus. She realized he was looking at her, and one evening she decided to take matters into her own hands. She walked up to him in the law school library and announced, "If you're going to keep looking at me, and I'm going to keep looking back, we might as well be introduced. I'm Hillary Rodham." For a moment, Bill was so surprised he couldn't remember his own name. He had met his match.

Bill and Hillary began to spend time together and talk. What Bill liked about her politics, he realized, was that "like me, she was both idealistic and practical." He was so smitten that at the end of the semester he gave up an opportunity to work on South Dakota senator George McGovern's presidential campaign to follow Hillary to her summer job at a California law firm. He loved her, he said, and wanted to see if things could work out between them. By the following fall, they were sharing a tiny apartment in New Haven, Connecticut.

But where would the relationship go from there? Bill Clinton knew what he wanted to do—return to Arkansas, get into politics, and run for governor. His home state, however, was rural and poor, with few opportunities for ambitious Yale lawyers. When she graduated, Hillary could have any high-profile job she wanted—in New York, Washington, D.C., San Francisco. Why would she want to go to Arkansas?

"I had met many of the ablest people of my generation," Bill wrote later, "and I thought [Hillary] was head and shoulders above them all in political potential. She had a big brain, a good heart, better organizational skills than I did, and political skills that were nearly as good as mine; I'd just had more experience. I loved her enough both to want her and to want the best for her. It was a high-class dilemma."

Sometime during the next few years, Hillary would have to make her decision. In the meantime, she stayed at law school for a fourth year and worked at the Yale Child Study Center so she and Bill could graduate together. In 1974, she received an offer she couldn't refuse: to work for the **House Judiciary Committee** in Washington, D.C., with thirty-nine other lawyers investigating the possible impeachment of President Richard Nixon. On July 19, the committee approved three articles of impeachment. On August 9, Nixon went on television and resigned the presidency.

From the moment they met, Bill Clinton and Hillary Rodham enjoyed each other's sharp intelligence and ready sense of humor.

Then, missing Bill terribly, Hillary decided to "follow her heart" and move to Arkansas in the fall of 1974. He was teaching law at the University of Arkansas in Fayetteville, and Hillary got a job there, too. She arrived just in time to help him run in his first race, for the U.S. House of Representatives, against popular Republican John Paul Hammerschmidt. Clinton crisscrossed the district with "boundless energy and enthusiasm," a fellow professor remembered, trying to greet every voter personally. As expected, he lost the November election—but by a very small margin, just 52 to 48 percent. Clearly, voters felt this young man had a bright future.

A Marriage of Equals

Bill had asked Hillary to marry him the year before, but she had needed time to think about it. Now, he tried to convince her again. While she was away on a trip, he went ahead and bought a little brick house she had admired. He picked her up at the airport on her return and drove by the house. "Now you better marry me because I can't live in it by myself," he told her. She agreed, and they set a date.

Hillary and Bill on their wedding day, October 11, 1975.

The night before the wedding, Hillary went to a local store with her mother and picked out a lace and muslin Victorian dress. On October 11, 1975, twenty-nine-year-old Bill Clinton and twenty-seven-year-old Hillary Rodham were married in the living room of their new home. After the ceremony, their friends threw them a big reception for three hundred guests.

Although she was married, Hillary Rodham decided to keep her own name. Bill's mother cried when she heard the news, and even Hillary's mother insisted on addressing her letters to "Mr. and Mrs. Bill Clinton." Hillary knew her decision would be controversial in Arkansas in the 1970s—but she didn't yet realize how controversial.

The couple's low-key life as law professors did not last long. In fall 1976, Bill was elected **attorney general** of Arkansas. He and Hillary moved again, this time to Little Rock, the state capital. Because he was now on the state payroll, his salary took a dive. Hillary realized that if Bill was going to stay in politics, she would have to be the primary wage earner. She took a job with the Rose Law Firm, one of the best-known firms in the state.

During his two-year term as attorney general, Bill developed a good reputation as an **activist** who fought for the rights of consumers. He had set his sights on a higher office, however, and when the Democratic governor of Arkansas decided to run for the U.S. Senate in 1978, Clinton seized the opportunity to seek his seat. He easily won both the Democratic **primary** and the November election against his Republican opponent, Lynn Lowe. At age thirty-two, Bill Clinton was the youngest governor in the nation. He had achieved the goal he had set for himself.

Governor in a Hurry

In his inaugural address, Clinton clearly stated his belief that the role of government was to work for the good of the general public. "For as long as I can remember," he said, "I have believed passionately in the cause of equal opportunity, and I will do what I can to advance it. . . . I have wished to ease the burdens of life for those who, through no fault of their own, are old or weak or in need, and I will try to help them. . . ."

Clinton wanted to get a lot done very fast. First on his agenda was the education system in Arkansas, ranked last in state spending. Clinton pushed through a 40 percent raise in state funding, including raises in teachers' salaries, money for textbooks and transportation, and programs for special education and for gifted and talented students. He also wanted a highway-repair program to fix Arkansas's old, damaged roads. To fund the program, the legislature passed a "car tag" bill increasing the cost of motor-vehicle registration tags. The plan damaged Clinton's popularity, especially in rural areas, when people suddenly found they had to pay twice as much to register their cars.

Hillary watches as Bill takes the oath of office in Little Rock, Arkansas, on January 9, 1979. At age thirty-two, he was the youngest governor in the nation.

The highlight of the Clintons' first two years in the governor's mansion was the birth of their daughter Chelsea Victoria on February 27, 1980. They named her after Joni Mitchell's song "Chelsea Morning," sung by folksinger Judy Collins. "Chelsea, this is new for both of us," Hillary told her newborn daughter one night when Chelsea wouldn't stop crying. "I've never been a mother before, and you've never been a baby. We're just going to have to help each other do the best we can."

Even before Chelsea was born, Hillary was thinking about her family's future. She knew that

Bill and Hillary pose with six-day-old Chelsea on March 5, 1980. Hillary described her daughter's birth as the "most miraculous event in our lives."

making money wasn't important to Bill, so if the family was going to have a "nest egg," it would be up to her to earn it. On a whim, she jumped into the extremely risky **commodities market**, made a lot of money in a short time, and then got out before she lost what she had earned. In addition, at the invitation of an Arkansas businessman named Jim McDougal, she and Bill invested money in a riverside property called Whitewater Estates. The plan was to divide the land into lots and sell them to people who wanted vacation homes. At the time, it seemed like a good investment.

In spring 1980, the governor found he had a political crisis on his hands. When thousands of Cuban refugees flooded into the United States, Democratic president Jimmy Carter sent twenty thousand of them to a camp in Fort Chafee, Arkansas. On May 26, about three hundred escaped and terrorized the neighboring towns. Clinton quickly dispatched the National Guard to recapture the Cubans, but many people blamed him for allowing the situation to develop.

In addition, voters were put off by the beards and long hair of Clinton's young, **liberal** staff and by Hillary's lack of interest in fashion and insistence on keeping her maiden name. To many, Bill seemed too young, too arrogant, and too out of touch with the people who had elected him. As a result, when Clinton ran for reelection in 1980, he lost by 52 to 48 percent—to a conservative Republican named Frank White.

Clinton was shocked and devastated. His once-shining future in politics seemed suddenly behind him. The family moved out of the governor's mansion and Bill took a new job at a local law firm, but his heart wasn't in it. Just one thing—besides his young daughter—cheered him up. The new governor wasn't popular after all. Clinton decided to run again.

A Political Comeback

Bill began his new campaign in February 1982 with an advertisement admitting his past mistakes and asking for another chance. Now he understood, he said, "You can't lead without listening." Hillary proved that she had been listening, too. This time, she went on the campaign trail under a new name—Hillary Rodham Clinton. "I decided that it was not an issue that was that big to me when it came right down to it," she admitted. She lightened her soft-brown hair color and styled it into a more becoming cut. The *Arkansas Gazette* noticed the change in Hillary Clinton approvingly: "She's softening her image a bit . . . and succeeding, apparently. She has become a good hand-shaking campaigner in the traditional Arkansas style."

Bill, Hillary, and Chelsea greet supporters at a parade in Little Rock, Arkansas, during Bill's race to regain the governorship in 1982.

After a hard-fought campaign, Bill Clinton beat White with 54.7 percent of the vote. He would win his next three elections and remain in office for the next ten years.

In that time, Bill tried to help the Arkansas people by improving the state's economy and job market. He would be proudest of his program to improve the state's education system— he appointed Hillary as head of an Education Standards Committee that suggested changes in the statewide curriculum.

By the late 1980s, Clinton had a national reputation as an able and effective governor. He was the driving force behind the Democratic Leadership Council, a **centrist** pro-business group in the Democratic Party. In 1988, he supported the Democratic presidential hopeful, Massachusetts governor Michael Dukakis, by giving the nominating speech at the Democratic convention. Unfortunately, Bill's long, rambling speech did not hold the attention of the delegates. Only when Clinton finally said, "In conclusion," did the weary audience applaud.

A few days later, Clinton managed to salvage his reputation by appearing on the late-night *Tonight Show* and exchanging one-liners with host Johnny Carson. He was only trying to make Dukakis look good, Bill joked, but he succeeded "beyond [his] wildest imagination." By the time he played saxophone with the studio band, the TV audience was on his side. Despite Clinton's efforts, Dukakis lost the election to Republican George H. W. Bush in November 1988.

Governor Bill Clinton announces his candidacy for the presidency during a speech in Little Rock, Arkansas, on October 3, 1991.

Presidential Dreams

On the morning of October 3, 1991, Clinton stood on the steps of the Old State House in Little Rock and announced that he was seeking the 1992 Democratic nomination for president. During the spring of that year, President Bush's approval rating had soared to an unprecedented 91 percent when the United States won the First Gulf War against Iraq. Then the economy took a downturn, and people started losing jobs. In addition, the amount of money the federal government borrowed and owed to individuals and institutions had quadrupled in the previous twelve years. This debt was primarily a result of tax cuts for wealthy people, rising health-care costs, and money spent on military defense. Bush was suddenly vulnerable.

So, it seemed, was Clinton. On February 4, 1992, an article in the supermarket tabloid *Star* claimed that an Arkansas woman named Gennifer Flowers had had an affair with Bill Clinton for twelve years, beginning in the late 1970s. Rumors about Clinton's extramarital affairs had swirled for a long time, and now the story was front-page news all over the country.

To tell their side of the story, the Clintons agreed to appear on the CBS-TV show *60 Minutes*. To interviewer Steve Kroft's insistent questions, Clinton admitted that he had caused "pain in my marriage."

Then, Hillary weighed in. "You know, I'm not sitting here, some little woman standing by my man like Tammy Wynette," she said. "I'm sitting here because I love him and I respect him and I honor what he's been through and what we've been through together."

The American people responded well to the frankness of the interview, and for the moment, the political damage was contained.

But Hillary would receive plenty of complaints about her remark, which seemed to mock country singer Tammy Wynette. Even more controversial was her awkward comment during another interview that "I suppose I could have stayed home and baked cookies and had teas, but what I decided to do was fulfill my profession." Her remark was interpreted as a criticism of homemakers.

Bill remained proud of his wife's accomplishments and liked to brag about her. When they were campaigning in New Hampshire, Clinton joked that by electing him, voters could "buy one, get one free." He and Hillary both expected her to take an active role in any possible Clinton administration.

Clinton's actions during the Vietnam War also surfaced during the campaign, and he had to protect himself against charges that he was a draft resister. When he attempted to explain himself, critics mocked him as "Slick Willie." However, he dubbed himself "The Comeback Kid" when he came in second in the New Hampshire primary on February 18.

Clinton went on to win enough delegates in the upcoming primaries to clinch the nomination. After the Democratic Convention in New York City in July 1992, Bill, Hillary, and vice-presidential running mate Al Gore and his wife

Endearing himself to the public, Bill Clinton plays the saxophone on "The Arsenio Hall Show" on June 3, 1992, during his campaign for the presidency. He never lost the love of music he developed as a child growing up in the rock 'n' roll era.

Clinton As a New Democrat

The Democratic Leadership Council that Clinton began chairing in 1990 was formed in 1985 during Republican Ronald Reagan's presidency. Leading Democrats wanted to develop centrist positions that would appeal to moderates and help Democrats regain the White House. Clinton supported such moderate policies as a balanced budget, free trade, health-care reform, and a more efficient, less-expensive government. As president, he would continue to support measures of which the more liberal members of the Democratic Party disapproved. For instance, in 1996, he signed a welfare reform bill that changed the way the federal government dispensed aid to poor and needy citizens. It included measures that encouraged able-bodied people to earn their own money instead of depending on the government for support.

Bill Clinton and his running mate Al Gore raise their hands to cheers from the crowd during the Democratic National Convention on July 16, 1992.

Tipper took off on a cross-country bus tour to bring their message to the American people: "Putting People First." Hillary jokingly called the group's trip "Bill, Al, Hillary, and Tipper's Excellent Adventure."

The election became a three-way contest when Texas billionaire Ross Perot jumped into the race, promising to erase the huge national debt that had grown during the terms of the last two Republican presidents. As Perot's popularity demonstrated, Bush's weakest point was clearly the country's troubled economy. To remind the staff of the key issue in the race, Clinton's campaign manager, James Carville, put up a sign in his headquarters that read: "It's the economy, stupid."

Apparently U.S. citizens thought so, too. On November 3, 1992, they elected William Jefferson Clinton president of the United States with 43 percent of the popular vote, compared to 37.4 percent for Bush and 19 percent for Perot. Clinton gained 370 **electoral votes** to 168 for Bush. When the results came in, Bill, Hillary, and Chelsea went over to the Old State House in Little Rock to greet the thousands of supporters swarming the streets. "This victory was more than a victory of party," Bill said. "It was a victory for those who work hard and play by the rules, a victory for people who felt left out and left behind and want to do better."

Bill and Hillary Clinton were going to the White House with a message of change.

During a televised debate at the University of Richmond, Virginia, on October 15, 1992, candidate Bill Clinton speaks forcefully while President George H. W. Bush (left) and independent candidate Ross Perot (right, sitting) look on. The debates highlighted Clinton's talent as a skilled public speaker.

CONTROVERSY AND CHANGE

On January 20, 1993, William Jefferson Clinton was sworn in as the forty-second president of the United States. "Today a generation raised in the shadows of the Cold War assumes new responsibilities in a world warmed by the sunshine of freedom but threatened still by ancient hatreds and new plagues. . . ." Clinton told the watching nation. "We must do what America does best: offer more opportunity to all and demand responsibility from all."

As Chelsea and Hillary look on, William Jefferson Clinton is sworn in as the forty-second president of the United States by Chief Justice William H. Rehnquist on January 20, 1993.

Political Struggles

The new administration got off to a shaky start. Clinton ran into immediate trouble trying to fulfill a campaign pledge to end the ban on gay and lesbian personnel in the U.S. military. In the face of conservative opposition, Clinton was forced to settle for a compromise "don't ask, don't tell" policy that satisfied no one.

Also, a standoff in Waco, Texas, between the Bureau of Alcohol, Tobacco, and Firearms (ATF) and a religious group, the Branch Davidians, ended in a fire in which more than eighty people died, including twenty-five children. Though new attorney general Janet Reno took full responsibility for the disastrous raid, the episode reflected badly on the president as well.

In keeping with his promise that he would "focus like a laser [beam] on the economy," Clinton proposed an economic package that both raised taxes and cut the cost of government. His tax bill included a large tax increase for wealthy people and for corporations, a tax deduction for working poor people, and a reduction of the federal government workforce. He even cut the White House staff by 25 percent. Even though the economy began to pick up in 1993, Republicans still criticized what they called the "largest tax increase in history."

Other Clinton victories included the Family and Medical Leave Act, which gave workers time off for family emergencies, and the Brady Bill, which mandated a five-day waiting period for handgun purchases.

By 1992, there were 37 million U.S. citizens without health insurance, and medical costs were continuing to skyrocket. Clinton announced that he was appointing Hillary to head a special task force to work on health-care reform. As Clinton aide Sidney Blumenthal pointed out, Hillary was the first wife of a president "who had the essential credentials to serve as a cabinet-level official." Hillary was pleased to take on the assignment.

Hillary Rodham Clinton introduces her health care plan during a visit to Johns Hopkins University in Baltimore, Maryland, on October 28, 1993. Despite a vigorous promotional campaign to explain it to the American people, the plan failed to win widespread support.

For months, Hillary and other experts studied the problem. They came up with a comprehensive set of programs that featured a network of health-care groups that would compete with each other. The 1,400-page bill was too lengthy and complicated for most people to grasp, however. In addition, other factors came to light, including the relative secrecy of the task force's meetings and its failure to consult Congress. Republican and medical insurance groups banded together in an effort to kill the plan. One insurance group aired a set of negative advertisements featuring a fictitious couple named Harry and Louise, who worried out loud about the proposed plans.

Dressed as Harry and Louise, Bill and Hillary spoofed the ad at the 1994 Gridiron dinner, an annual event for reporters. "It says here on page 3,764 that under the Clinton health security plan, we could get sick," Hillary said with mock alarm.

"That's terrible," Bill said, shaking his head.

"And look at this, it gets worse," Hillary said. "On page 12,743—no, I got that wrong—on page 27,655, it says that eventually we're all going to die!"

Although they laughed about it, the health-care plan was doomed. The Clintons were never able to muster enough support, and in September 1994, the bill died without ever coming to a vote.

Clinton had come into office facing a Republican majority in both the **House of Representatives** and the Senate. The Republicans badly wanted to gain control, and in fall 1994 they rallied behind House Minority Leader Newt Gingrich, who wrote a ten-point program dubbed the "Contract with America." The program included measures dear to conservatives' hearts, including an increase in defense spending, a cut in taxes for wealthy citizens, and stiffer penalties for criminals. On Election Day 1994, the Republicans won enough seats to capture control of the Senate (52–48) and the House (230–204). For the first time in forty years, Republicans controlled the Congress. Now it would be harder than ever for Clinton to get his own programs passed.

At Home in the White House

The first thing Bill Clinton had done when he moved into the White House was to take his mother to see the Rose Garden, where he had shaken hands with President Kennedy so many years before. Then, the family had to get used to living there.

Hillary redecorated the little kitchen in the residence, so that the family could get together for casual dinners. Also, she turned the sunroom on the third floor into a big family room where they could watch television, play card games, and talk with friends and family. Despite his late nights, Clinton tried to fit in a jog every morning. His favorite route was to run along the National Mall to the Lincoln Memorial and the Capitol and back. Soon, for reasons of security, the Secret Service put an end to the public runs.

The Clintons are the very picture of family togetherness as they leave the White House on November 26, 1997. They spent Thanksgiving at the presidential retreat at Camp David, Maryland.

Hillary came into the White House expecting to perform the job traditionally assigned to first ladies—host social events—and also to work on domestic policy, especially "issues affecting women, children, and families." For this reason, she requested that her staff have offices not only in the East Wing of the White House, where first ladies traditionally have their offices, but also in the president's West Wing. Soon, Hillary's space within the White House was known as "Hillaryland."

Hillary was a bit nervous about her social duties but determined to "put her own stamp on the White House, as previous First Couples had done." First, she decided the White House should feature American foods and wines. At Christmas, she made American crafts her theme and decorated Christmas trees with handmade wood ornaments made by artists from across the country.

Chelsea Clinton was just twelve years old when her father became president. She would spend her teenage years in the

White House, and Bill and Hillary wanted to protect her as much as possible from the loss of privacy. Shortly after the inauguration, Hillary had a long talk with former First Lady Jackie Kennedy, who had successfully raised two children in the public spotlight. "Don't spoil her," Jackie warned Hillary. "Don't let her think she's someone special or entitled. Keep the press away from her if you can, and don't let anyone use her." The Clintons had already decided to send Chelsea to Sidwell Friends School, a local private school where she would be protected from the news media.

Throughout her White House years, the press mostly kept their pledge to leave Chelsea alone. As the daughter of the president, she traveled around the world, often going on official visits with her parents. Chelsea grew up to be bright, inquisitive, and poised. Whatever they might have thought of her parents, critics and fans alike agreed that the Clintons did a wonderful job of raising their daughter.

Foreign Matters

When Clinton became president, he inherited a very serious foreign-policy problem in Eastern Europe. After the Cold War ended in 1990, much of former Yugoslavia split into three warring divisions torn apart by **ethnic** and religious differences: Serbs (Eastern Orthodox Christians), Croatians (Catholics), and Bosnians (Muslims).

End of the Cold War

For the second half of the twentieth century, the United States was engaged in the Cold War with the Union of Soviet Socialist Republics (U.S.S.R), a Communist nation made up of fifteen republics that also controlled most Eastern European nations. By the end of the 1980s, the Soviet economy was collapsing, the republics were demanding independence, and countries in Eastern Europe were rejecting their communist leaders. Communism fell in East Germany, Poland, Czechoslovakia, Romania, Hungary, and Bulgaria. Russia, the largest and most powerful republic within the Soviet Union, elected its own president, Boris Yeltsin. Finally, in December 1991, the Soviet Union was dissolved. The United States had won the Cold War.

President Clinton visits a U.S. Army base in Tuzla, Bosnia, on January 13, 1996. After the Dayton Peace Accord was signed, seven thousand American troops were sent to Bosnia to join with other NATO forces in keeping the peace.

As part of his campaign to create a "Greater Serbia" in the region, in 1992 former Communist leader Slobodan Milosevic backed Serbian militants who launched full-scale warfare in Bosnia. Bosnian Serbs turned against their Muslim neighbors and began a widespread killing of civilians. In February 1994, Clinton called for the North Atlantic Treaty Organization (NATO) to protect the Muslims.

Determined to gain a permanent cease-fire, Clinton held a peace summit at an air force base in Dayton, Ohio, where the leaders of the three factions were pressured to come to an agreement. On December 14, 1995, the Dayton Peace Accords were signed, and Clinton committed U.S. troops to help NATO forces keep the peace. It was a very successful effort. In his State of the Union address on January 23, 1996, Clinton was able to say proudly, "We stood up for peace in Bosnia. Remember the skeletal prisoners, the mass graves, the campaign to rape and torture . . . all these horrors have now begun to give way to the promise of peace."

Clinton also took steps to end the long-standing conflict between the Jewish nation of Israel and mostly Muslim Palestinians in the Middle East. He pushed Israel and the Palestinian Authority to meet in Oslo, Norway, for months of talks about disputes over territory and to draw up a time line for gradual Israeli withdrawal from the regions of the Gaza Strip and the West Bank. Then in September 1993, he invited Israeli leader Yitzhak Rabin and Palestine Liberation

Bill Clinton encourages a handshake between Israeli Prime Minister Yitzhak Rabin (left) and Palestine Liberation Organization chairman Yasser Arafat (right) after the signing of the peace accord between Israel and the Palestinians on September 13, 1993.

Organization (PLO) leader Yasser Arafat to Washington to sign the Oslo Accords. At the signing ceremony on September 13, Clinton even persuaded Rabin and Arafat to shake hands. Clinton felt that the peace accords were a good step in the right direction, but tragically in 1995, Rabin was assassinated by a **right-wing** Jewish fanatic, and the timetable slowed down.

The Clinton Scandals

From the beginning of their time in the White House, the Clintons were subjected to a barrage of criticism. Hillary found herself under a magnifying glass. The press criticized her hair styles, her clothes, her office in the West Wing, her handling of the health-care proposal.

It was Bill Clinton, though, who really "[made] the Republicans crazy," as one reporter quipped. Many conservatives were annoyed that despite the allegations of affairs and draft resistance that had surfaced during the campaign, Clinton had still beaten Bush. In the first year of his presidency, supposed Clinton scandals were unearthed monthly and broadcast in newspapers and on cable television and radio talk shows: mysterious firings in the White House travel office (Travelgate); Bill's $200 hair cut (Hairgate); the misuse of FBI files (Filegate). On Father's Day 1993, the *Washington Post* revealed that Clinton's father had been married up to three other times and that Bill had at least one more half brother and a half sister. It came as a shock.

Suspicions continued to surface that the Clintons had been involved in wrongdoing in the failed Whitewater land development deal, on which they lost about $65,000. Their old partner Jim McDougal had since been charged in a savings-and-loan bank scandal, and rumors flew that the Clintons had somehow had something to do with that, too.

On July 20, 1993, six months after Clinton took office, his old childhood friend and White House lawyer, Vincent Foster, committed suicide, and Whitewater files were taken from his office by presidential aides. Some Clinton opponents were immediately suspicious and circulated rumors that Foster had been murdered and that his death had something to do with Whitewater. Republicans in Congress began to demand that a special prosecutor investigate Whitewater. In January 1994, Clinton agreed to the appointment. It was a decision he would come to deeply regret.

Then, in May 1994, a former Arkansas State employee named Paula Jones filed a civil lawsuit claiming she had been sexually harassed by Clinton five years before, while he was still governor. His attorneys argued the lawsuit should be put off until after Clinton left office. They took their case all the way to the Supreme Court in May 1997. The court ruled against the president, asserting that the case wouldn't take much time. They would be proved wrong.

A Second Term

Meanwhile, Clinton was coming up for reelection in 1996. The Republican takeover of Congress hadn't gone as well as Newt Gingrich had planned. When a battle over the budget shut down the government in both November and December 1995, more than eight hundred thousand government workers were sent home, and the public blamed the Republicans.

Bill Clinton and Republican challenger Bob Dole discuss issues in a televised debate in San Diego, California, on October 16, 1996.

The economy continued on its upward swing—the federal debt was going down and unemployment had fallen to 5.6 percent. Clinton's approval ratings were about 60 percent. At the Democratic Convention in Chicago at the end of August 1996, Clinton sounded the optimistic slogan of his campaign: "We need to build a bridge to the future . . . let us resolve to build that bridge to the twenty-first century." This time, he was running against **Senate Majority Leader** Robert Dole of Kansas, a respected World War II veteran with a good sense of humor and poor campaign skills. Dole's jokes couldn't save him, and on election day 1996, Clinton won a second term with 379 electoral votes compared to Dole's 159. Bill Clinton was the first Democrat to be elected to a second term since Franklin D. Roosevelt in 1936.

CHAPTER FIVE

A PRESIDENCY ON THE EDGE

Despite the ongoing Whitewater investigation, the Clintons started their second term with high hopes. At his State of the Union message on February 4, 1997, Clinton laid out his bridge to the twenty-first century: welfare reform, a balanced budget, education reform. For her part, Hillary hoped to be able to continue her behind-the-scenes work on women's and children's issues, both at home and abroad.

Whitewater prosecutor Ken Starr talks to reporters about his ongoing investigation on January 22, 1998. Although Starr promised that his investigation would not be motivated by politics, many observers argued that it in fact was.

Meanwhile, the Whitewater investigations continued. After four years, special investigator Kenneth Starr and the **Office of Independent Counsel** had been unable to find evidence linking the Clintons to anything illegal in any of the Whitewater investigations. The investigators and many Republicans in Congress believed that the evidence was there if only they could find it, however. The Clintons had handed over decades worth of records; government employees had combed through millions of documents; and White House staff, members of the administration, and even Secret Service agents were being called to testify.

The case consumed the Clintons in private. "We talked about it all the time," Clinton revealed later. "We thought it was just crazy." In public, however, Clinton appeared confident, in control, and on the job. As for Hillary, she had realized long before the truth of former First Lady Eleanor Roosevelt's remark that every woman in public life must "develop skin as tough as rhinoceros hide."

Shaking his finger, President Clinton states unequivocally that he did not have improper relations with "that woman, Miss Lewinsky," in a televised speech on January 26, 1998. His boldfaced lie would come back to haunt him.

Public Shame and Private Trauma

Then, on January 21, 1998, a bombshell dropped. The front page of the *Washington Post* featured a story alleging that Bill Clinton had had an affair with a young White House intern named Monica Lewinsky. Immediately, Clinton denied the accusations: to his wife, to his staff, to his friends, and to the country. In front of a television audience, he pointed his finger at the camera and said angrily, "I want to say one thing to the American people. . . . I did not have sexual relations with that woman, Ms. Lewinsky." Now the news was all Monica, all the time.

Although she knew her husband had been unfaithful in the past, Hillary believed his story. Surely he would not have been so reckless as to risk his presidency and his marriage by carrying on an affair while in office. On January 27, she appeared on NBC's *Today* show and publicly defended him. "I have learned a long time ago that the only people who count in any marriage are the two that are in it," she stated forcefully. Besides, she told interviewer Matt Lauer, "I guess I've just been through it so many times. I mean, Bill and I have been accused of everything, including murder, [by] some of the very same people who are behind these allegations. [So] from my perspective, this is part of the continuing political campaign against my husband." She characterized the attacks as coming from a "vast right-wing conspiracy."

White House photographers caught this image of President Clinton hugging Monica Lewinsky on a rope line at a White House lawn party on November 6, 1996.

Four months later, an Arkansas judge dismissed the Paula Jones case as having no legal merit, but the damage had already been done. On January 17, 1998, Clinton had given evidence to lawyers in the case. Under oath, he denied having any inappropriate physical contact with intern Monica Lewinsky. Only Clinton and his prosecutors knew that his statement was a lie.

On August 6, 1998, Monica Lewinsky testified to the Starr team. On August 17, the president testified as well. This time, under oath, he admitted he had had "inappropriate intimate contact" with the White House intern. That night, he went on TV and admitted the truth to the American people. His behavior was wrong, he said, but it was time to move on. "Now, this matter is between me, the two people I love most—my wife and our daughter—and our God. I must put it right, and I am prepared to do whatever it takes to do so."

Clinton knew he may have wrecked his marriage. On August 15, early in the morning, he had woken Hillary and told her he had lied. It was, Hillary recalled afterwards, "the most devastating, shocking, and hurtful experience of my life." The day after Bill's testimony, the family left for a planned vacation in Martha's Vineyard in Massachusetts. Stiffly, in full view of the TV cameras, they walked to the helicopter on the White House lawn. Chelsea acted as the buffer between her parents, holding each of them by the hand but leaning close to her mother. Hillary, hidden behind dark glasses, would not even look at Bill. "Clearly, this is not the best day in Mrs. Clinton's life," her press secretary said in a prepared statement. "But her love for him is compassionate and steadfast."

Hillary, Chelsea, Bill, and their dog Buddy make the long walk across the White House lawn to a waiting helicopter on August 18, 1998, just three days after Bill told his wife he had been unfaithful. Bill said later that the only person talking to him that morning was Buddy.

For weeks, a furious and humiliated Hillary barely spoke to her husband. They began marriage counseling to see whether the relationship could be saved. Through the counseling, Bill wrote afterwards, "Hillary and I . . . got to know each other again, beyond the work and ideas we shared and the child we adored. I had always loved her very much, but not always very well. . . . We were still each other's best friend, and I hoped we could save our marriage."

Gradually Hillary did come to the realization that she still loved Bill and wanted the marriage to continue. In the meantime, her popularity with the public soared, as people admired her grace under pressure and her decision to "stand by her man." Amazingly, they also continued to rate the president's job performance—though not his personal morality—highly. Just four days after his televised appearance, an ABC poll rated the president's job approval rating at 64 percent.

Speaker of the House Newt Gingrich hoped that the scandals would make the president so unpopular that the Democrats would be swept out of office in the 1998 congressional elections. In the actual election, however, Democrats gained five House seats and retained all of their Senate seats. No longer trusted by his party, Gingrich resigned as speaker. Most people, it seemed, found the scandal coverage excessive and embarrassing, and disapproved of the way the Republicans were handling it.

A Historic Debate

Nonetheless, the Office of Independent Counsel moved ahead and sent a recommendation for impeachment to the House Judiciary Committee. According to the Constitution, the House of Representatives can impeach, or formally charge, a president for crimes committed in office. If a majority chooses to impeach, then the case goes to the Senate, where two-thirds of the members must vote guilty in order for a president to be convicted and removed from office. Only serious crimes having to do with the nation— "Treason, Bribery, or other high Crimes and misdemeanors"— qualify as grounds for impeachment.

The president had lied under oath about a sexual affair— arguably a private, not a public, offense. Did it rate as a "high crime or misdemeanor"? In an open letter published in newspapers throughout the country, four hundred well-known American historians argued that it didn't. "We urge you, whether you are a Republican, a Democrat, or an Independent," they stated, "to oppose the dangerous new theory of impeachment, and to demand the restoration of the normal operations of our federal government."

Most Democrats, appalled and angered by the president's actions, favored a vote to censure, or reprimand, him as the most appropriate punishment. Republicans, however, demanded

Impeachment

The Founding Fathers set the bar very high for impeachment and removal from office to prevent Congress from getting rid of presidents just because they disagree with them politically.

President Andrew Johnson became president on April 15, 1865, when Lincoln was assassinated after the Civil War. A moderate Republican from Tennessee, Johnson attempted to block the efforts of a group called the **Radical** Republicans to punish the former Confederate states and ensure equal rights to freed slaves. They vowed to get rid of Johnson, and their excuse came when he seemed to violate federal law by removing the secretary of war from office.

Three days later, on February 24, 1868, Johnson was impeached by the House of Representatives and his case went to trial in the Senate. Johnson's lawyers insisted that his actions did not constitute an impeachable offense. Finally, the Senate found him not guilty by a vote of 35 to 19, just one vote less than a two-thirds majority. Johnson had narrowly escaped conviction by a single vote.

impeachment, and on November 19, 1998, Kenneth Starr testified to the House Judiciary Committee. In the course of his testimony, he acknowledged that in his lengthy, $45 million investigation, he had found no evidence to charge the Clintons on Whitewater—the original matter under investigation.

Even so, on December 19, 1998, Bill Clinton was impeached by the House on two counts—for perjury, or lying under oath, and for obstruction of justice. While most Republicans voted for impeachment, most Democrats voted against it. Thus William Jefferson Clinton became only the second president of the United States, after Andrew Johnson, to be impeached.

For five weeks in early 1999, the Senate tried Clinton on the two charges. Dale Bumpers, a former senator from Arkansas, made the summary argument for the defense. He reminded the senators of what the Founding Fathers had written in *The Federalist* papers—impeachment was appropriate only for a "*political* offense" against the nation. "Even perjury, concealing or deceiving an unfaithful relationship, does not even come close to being an impeachable offense," Bumpers said. "Nobody has suggested that Bill Clinton has committed a political crime against the state." In the end, the Senate voted 55 to 45 to **acquit** Clinton on charges of committing perjury, and 51 to 50 to acquit him on charges of obstruction of justice. On February 11, 1999, Chief Justice William Rehnquist, who presided over the trial, announced that William Jefferson Clinton was "acquitted of the charges in the said articles."

This *New York Times* headline on February 13, 1999, trumpets the news of President Clinton's acquittal on charges of perjury and obstruction of justice.

The spectacle was over. Even his friends agreed that Clinton's own reckless and immoral behavior had given his enemies the weapon they needed to almost destroy his presidency. The final responsibility was his.

Five years later, on June 26, 2004, *Time* magazine published an article on the occasion of the release of Bill Clinton's autobiography titled *My Life*. The article claimed that "In retrospect, it is clear that there was no substance to the Whitewater allegations and the other White House scandalettes—the travel-office firings, the FBI files, the death of Vincent Foster—except, of course, Lewinsky." History, however, will be the final judge of the Clinton scandals.

Seeking Peace at Home and Abroad

Even while Clinton was dealing with the unfolding scandal, foreign affairs claimed his urgent attention. Terrorism became an

A man is pulled to safety after the terrorist bombing of the U.S. embassy in Nairobi, Kenya, on August 7, 1998. The blast killed more than 100 people and injured more than 1,600, most of them Kenyans.

increasing concern throughout the 1990s. On February 26, 1993, radical Muslim terrorists set off a car bomb at the World Trade Center in New York City. The Central Intelligence Agency (CIA) began to track Osama bin Laden, a wealthy Saudi Arabian who planned and financed a global terrorist network named al-Qaeda. After bin Laden called for terrorist attacks on "American military and civilian targets anywhere in the world," al-Qaeda agents struck at U.S. embassies in the African countries of Tanzania and Kenya in August

1998, killing 257 people. Clinton realized the time had come to kill or capture bin Laden.

The CIA received word that bin Laden and some of his top agents were meeting in Afghanistan, and Clinton decided to strike. On August 20, 1998—just three days after his public confession on national television—Clinton ordered the bombing of the Afghan site. But bin Laden was not there. Reports said he had slipped out just hours before the missiles struck. Clinton realized the nation would be involved in a long, continuous struggle against terrorism. Although the United States prevented any terrorist strikes on "Y2K"—the widely-celebrated start of the new millennium on January 1, 2000—al-Qaeda bombed the American naval **destroyer** USS *Cole* in Aden, Yemen, ten months later, on October 12, 2000. Later, Clinton would tell president-elect George W. Bush that the thing he most regretted about his presidency was not getting bin Laden.

On October 22, 2000, a boat filled with explosives pulled up beside the USS *Cole* in the port of Aden, Yeman. The boat blew this hole in the side of the USS *Cole*, killing seventeen American sailors.

During the last year of his presidency, Clinton flew around the world trying to negotiate peace in places as distant as Pakistan, India, Northern Ireland, and the Middle East. He pushed Yasser Arafat hard to sign a peace deal that would establish a Palestinian state in return for granting certain rights to Israel. The Israeli government agreed to the historic deal, but Arafat hemmed and hawed and delayed, and Clinton had to leave office without the wide-ranging peace plan he had worked so hard to bring about. Arafat's failure would have tragic consequences for the region.

Clinton's military campaign in the Serbian province of Kosovo had a much better outcome. In 1998, Slobodan Milosevic started a military operation against the Kosovar Albanians, who sought independence from Serbia. The Serbian Army raged through Kosovo, burning towns, murdering civilians, and driving 1.5 million people from their homes. On March 23, 1999, after repeated attempts to negotiate peace had failed, the United States and its

NATO allies began air strikes against military and economic targets in Serbia. By June, after 30,000 bombing missions, Serbian forces were finally forced out of Kosovo. Under Clinton's leadership, the NATO alliance was an overwhelming success, and **genocide** was halted.

"Don't Stop Thinking About Tomorrow"

As Bill's presidency wound down, new opportunities opened up for Hillary. In November 1998, the long-time Democratic senator from

Hillary Rodham Clinton officially announces her candidacy for the U.S. Senate on February 6, 2000. Hillary's mother, Dorothy Rodham, Chelsea, and Bill look on (seated first, second, and third from right).

New York, Daniel Patrick Moynihan, announced his retirement as of 2000. Hillary's friends tried to persuade her to run for his seat. True, she was not a New York native, but that might not matter to New Yorkers, who had welcomed immigrants for four hundred years—and might also welcome a world-famous first lady.

At first, Hillary was worried about whether she had the energy and will to run and win. Later, she would write, "The most difficult decisions I have made in my life were to stay married to Bill and to run for the Senate from New York." As she and Bill talked over the possibility, he encouraged her to take the chance. In order to establish residency, they bought an 1880s farmhouse in the Westchester town of Chappaqua.

Then, on July 7, 1999, she began her "listening tour" of the state. "I think I have some real work to do to get out and listen and learn from the people of New York," she said, "and demonstrate that what I'm for is maybe as important, if not more important, than where I'm from." Her tour took her from Buffalo in northwest New York State to Long Island in the south. By the time she was officially nominated as the Democratic candidate in May 2000, Hillary was an expert on the economic problems of northern New York and the environmental concerns of Long Islanders.

Hillary's first Republican opponent, New York mayor Rudolph Giuliani, dropped out of the race for personal reasons in May 2000, and she found herself facing Long Island congressman Rick Lazio in the fall election. Relatively young and inexperienced, Lazio tried to capitalize on distrust of Hillary among conservative voters. A Republican fund-raising letter said that Lazio's message could be summed up in just six words: "I'm running against Hillary Rodham Clinton."

"New Yorkers deserve more than that," Hillary shot back. "How about seven words: jobs, education, health, Social Security, environment, choice?"

On Election Day 2000, the Clintons celebrated as Hillary won a solid victory—55 percent of the vote to Lazio's 43 percent. "Sixty-two counties, sixteen months, three debates, two opponents, and six black pantsuits later, because of you, we are here!" an exuberant Hillary told her supporters.

Hillary and Chelsea celebrate Hillary's victory against Republican rival Rick Lazio on November 7, 2000. Hillary Rodham Clinton became the first woman ever to serve as a United States senator from New York.

Two-and-a-half months later, the Clintons hosted a party on the East Lawn to thank all the people who had worked at the White House for the past eight years. After a conflict-ridden election, Republican George W. Bush had beaten Vice President Al Gore to become the new president of the United States. In a few weeks, the Clintons would be gone. As a surprise, the band Fleetwood Mac came to the party and began to sing Clinton's theme song, "Don't Stop Thinking About Tomorrow." Bill and Hillary sang along with the rest.

One of the most interesting—and controversial—presidencies in U.S. history was over.

THE ULTIMATE POWER COUPLE

In 2000, First Lady Hillary Clinton became Senator Clinton, and President Clinton became just plain Bill. Before leaving office, though, Clinton had already started planning what he would do when his presidency ended. Like other past presidents, he would build a presidential library—Clinton's would be in Little Rock, Arkansas—and work on his memoirs. Even so, the first few months of his new life in Chappaqua were difficult, especially with Hillary on the job full time down in Washington, D.C.

Then, Clinton started traveling. Extremely popular internationally while he was president, he met with huge, enthusiastic crowds wherever he went. In April 2001, he journeyed to India to visit victims of a devastating earthquake. "Cleen-ton! Cleen-ton!" the enormous crowd chanted. In South Africa, he was enthusiastically greeted by former South African president Nelson Mandela. A month later, in Ireland, he was practically mobbed by admirers.

In July 2001, Clinton officially opened the offices of the new William J. Clinton Presidential Foundation in Harlem in New York City. From there, he planned to coordinate with other foundations and nations to "meet the challenges of global independence." Areas of special emphasis would include AIDS research and prevention and programs to help poor people help themselves.

In April 2001, Bill Clinton visited Anjar, India, the site of an earthquake in which twenty thousand people were killed. He helped organize aid for the survivors.

Becoming a Senator

Hillary Clinton knew she was a controversial figure on Capitol Hill, and she began her Senate term by keeping a deliberately low profile. Soon, though, she had impressed her colleagues with her dedication, knowledge, and willingness to compromise. She had

September 11, 2001

At 8:45 A.M. on September 11, 2001, a hijacked American Airlines plane flew into the North Tower of the World Trade Center in New York City. Just eighteen minutes later, another hijacked plane, United Airlines Flight 175, crashed into the South Tower. The United States was under attack. As more than 10,000 gallons (37,854 liters) of burning jet fuel pushed the temperatures in the skyscrapers as high as 2,000 degrees Fahrenheit (1,096 Celsius), their internal steel structure melted.

One after the other, the 110-story towers collapsed, turning the World Trade Center site into a smoking heap of rubble. The attacks on the World Trade Center were part of a coordinated attack by the Muslim terrorist group al-Qaeda. The Twin Towers were not the only targets. That morning, at 9:43 A.M., American Airlines Flight 77 crashed into the Pentagon, the headquarters of the U.S. military in Virginia. Also, United Flight 92 crashed into a field in western Pennsylvania after passengers fought with hijackers for control of the plane. Investigators believe that if the passengers hadn't rebelled, the hijackers might have smashed the plane into either the White House or the Capitol in Washington, D.C. Altogether, 2,792 people were killed in the Twin Towers, 125 in the Pentagon, and 265 in the four airliners, including 19 hijackers.

expected to concentrate on women's and children's issues and improving the upstate New York economy. Then came the terrorist attacks on September 11, 2001.

Early on the morning of September 12, Senator Clinton flew into New York City by helicopter and caught her first glimpse of the World Trade Center site by air. Ground Zero, as the site was called, looked like "the Gates of Hell," she said afterward. "I was totally unprepared for what I saw. The damage, the mountain of burning wreckage, the smell, just was overwhelming." From that moment, she said, responding to the emergency and fighting terrorism became "the primary obligation[s] of my term." With New York senator Charles Schumer, she procured a promise of $20 million in federal aid for cleanup and reconstruction, and she requested

Senator Clinton talks with firefighters and rescue workers at the World Trade Center disaster site on September 20, 2001.

a seat as the first New York member of the important Senate Armed Services Committee. On October 11, 2002, she voted to give President George W. Bush authority to go to war in Iraq. During Thanksgiving 2003, Senator Clinton traveled overseas to visit troops in Afghanistan and Iraq.

Hillary hugs Bill after introducing him at the Democratic National Convention in Boston on July 6, 2004. The former president gave a speech in support of Democratic presidential nominee John Kerry.

Into the Future

Bill did whatever he could to support his wife. To sustain their long-distance relationship, he flies to Washington during the week, and she spends long weekends in Chappaqua. In between, they talk to each other a lot on the phone. Five years after the crisis that almost ended their marriage, Bill Clinton said, "We're still laughing, having a good time together."

In early September 2004, the Clintons experienced a scare when doctors discovered that Bill had life-threatening heart disease. In quadruple bypass surgery on September 6, doctors took blood vessels from other parts of his body and attached them to his arteries so that blood could flow around the clogged areas. As tens of thousands of get-well messages poured in, Hillary admitted, "The past few days have been quite an emotional roller coaster." Luckily, Bill recovered according to schedule.

Despite the many challenges facing them both, the Clintons have remained a force in U.S. politics. Hillary has continued to make a name for herself in the Senate and has plans to run for reelection in 2006, backed by a proud Bill Clinton. Polls have also shown that Hillary would gain support in a bid for president. "I'm so proud of her," Bill has said. "I'm grateful that after all the help she gave me . . . I can now support her."

1946	William Jefferson Blythe III born on August 19
1947	Hillary Rodham born on October 26
1962	Bill Blythe changes his name to Bill Clinton
1963	Bill attends Boys Nation in Washington, D.C., and meets President John F. Kennedy
1964	Bill attends Georgetown University
1966	Hillary goes to Wellesley College
1968	Bill attends Oxford University on a Rhodes scholarship
1969	Hillary gives commencement address at Wellesley; *Life* magazine names Hillary as one of the nation's new young leaders; in fall she enters Yale Law School
1970	Bill enrolls at Yale Law School
1971	Bill and Hillary meet at Yale Law School
1974	Hillary is on House Judiciary Committee; President Richard Nixon resigns August 9; Bill loses race for House of Representatives
1975	Bill and Hillary marry on October 11
1976	Bill is elected attorney general of Arkansas
1977	Hillary joins Rose Law Firm
1978	Bill is elected governor of Arkansas
1980	Chelsea Victoria Clinton is born on February 27; Bill is defeated for reelection as governor
1982	Bill is reelected as governor of Arkansas
1992	Bill Clinton is elected president on November 3
1993	Muslim terrorists bomb World Trade Center February 26; Vince Foster commits suicide July 20; Yitzhak Rabin and Yasser Arafat sign peace accord on September 13
1994	Whitewater investigation begins in January; Hillary's health-care plan defeated
1995	Treaty ends war in Bosnia on December 14; government shuts down over budget battles in both November and December; Paula Jones files lawsuit against Clinton
1996	Bill signs welfare reform bill law on August 22; Bill reelected on November 5
1998	Lewinsky scandal revealed in January; Bill admits relationship on August 17; Bill impeached by House of Representatives on December 19; U.S. Embassy in Kenya bombed by terrorists
1999	Bill Clinton acquitted by Senate on February 11; United States and NATO begin air war over Kosovo in March
2000	Al-Qaeda bombs the USS *Cole* on October 12; Hillary Rodham Clinton elected senator from New York; George W. Bush elected president
2001	The Muslim terrorist group al-Qaeda attacks the United States on September 11
2004	Bill's autobiography *My Life* is published; Bill has heart surgery on September 6

GLOSSARY

acquit—free from charges; declare not guilty.

activist—person who tries to bring about social or political change through active involvement.

attorney general—chief law enforcement officer of a state or nation.

centrist—someone who supports ideas that fall evenly between two opposing positions.

commodities market—a financial exchange for buying and selling goods for future profit.

communist—pertaining to a government in which one political party holds power and all property is owned by the government or the community as a whole.

conservative—viewpoint that supports traditional values or institutions and does not favor taking chances or risks.

deferment—the postponement of an obligation or agreement until a future time.

destroyer—small, fast warship.

draft—the process by which the U.S. government recruits young male citizens for military service.

draft cards—forms used to register men for military service during war.

electoral votes—the votes for president and vice president submitted by representatives from each state, based on the popular vote in each state.

ethnic—relating to a group of people with their own language, history, or culture.

genocide—the intentional attempt to exterminate all members of a certain race, nationality, or cultural group.

House Judiciary Committee—part of the United States House of Representatives charged with overseeing legal matters.

House Minority Leader—person who heads the political party (Democrat or Republican) which has the least members in the House of Representatives and so does not control it.

House of Representatives—lower house of the United States Congress. The number of representatives from each state is determined by the state's population.

impeach—to formally charge a public official with misconduct in public office.

liberal—viewpoint favoring progress and change in government; or a person who holds such a view.

migrant camps—outdoor areas where temporary shelters are established for people who travel from place to place to find employment, especially farm workers.

moderate—person who does not favor extreme political or social ideas, positions, or actions.

Office of Independent Counsel—group of special prosecutors who investigate alleged crimes or impeachable conduct by some high government officials.

primary—early election in which members of each political party vote for a candidate to run for president in the general election.

radical—viewpoint that favors extreme changes in politics or society.

right-wing—those within a political group who are the most extreme about maintaining established traditions or policies.

Senate—the upper house of the United States Congress. Each state in the union is represented by two senators.

Senate Majority Leader—person who heads the political party (Democrat or Republican) which has the most members in the Senate and so is in control of it.

Speaker of the House—person who heads the political party (Democrat or Republican) which has the most members in the U.S. House of Representatives and so is in control of it.

FURTHER INFORMATION

Further Reading

Aaseng, Nathan. *The Impeachment of Bill Clinton*. (Famous Trials). San Diego: Lucent Books, 2000.

Corzine, Phyllis. *The Palestinian-Israeli Accord*. (Lucent Overview Series). Chicago: Greenhaven Press, 1997.

Frank, Mitch. *Understanding September 11th: Answering Questions About the Attacks on America*. New York: Viking Children's Books, 2002.

Gormley, Beatrice. *First Ladies: Women Who Called the White House Home*. Madison, WI: Turtleback Books, 2004.

Hakim, Joy. *All the People, 1945-1999*. (A History of Us, Vol. 10). New York: Oxford University Press, 1999.

Hampton, Wilborn. *September 11, 2001: Attack on New York City: Interviews and Accounts*. Cambridge, MA: Candlewick, 2003.

Harris, Nathaniel. *Israel and the Arab Nations in Conflict*. (New Perspectives). London: Hodder Wayland, 1998.

Haugen, David M. *The Vietnam War*. (American War Library). San Diego: Lucent Books, 2002.

Heinrichs, Ann. *William Jefferson Clinton*. (Profiles of the Presidents). Minneapolis: Compass Point Books, 2002.

Howard, Todd. *William Clinton*. (Presidents and Their Decisions). Chicago: Greenhaven Press, 2000.

Kendall, Martha. *Failure is Impossible!: The History of American Women's Rights*. (People's History). Minneapolis: Lerner Publishing Group, 2001.

Kent, Deborah. *Hillary Rodham Clinton: 1947*. (Encyclopedia of First Ladies). New York: Children's Press, 1999.

Mayo, Edith P. (ed.) *The Smithsonian Book of First Ladies: Their Lives, Times, and Issues*. New York: Henry Holt/ Smithsonian Institute Press, 1996.

Ryan, Bernard Jr. *Hillary Rodham Clinton: First Lady and Senator*. (Ferguson Career Biographies). New York: Facts on File, 2004.

Schuman, Michael A. *Bill Clinton*. (United States Presidents). Springfield, NJ: Enslow, 2003.

Taylor, David. *The Cold War*. (Twentieth Century Perspectives). Chicago: Heinemann Library, 2001.

Taylor, David. *The Wars of Former Yugoslavia*. (The Troubled World). Chicago: Heinemann-Raintree, 2003.

Wagner, Heather Lehr. *Hillary Rodham Clinton*. (Women in Politics). New York: Chelsea House, 2004.

FURTHER INFORMATION

Places to Visit

Clinton Birthplace Foundation
117 South Hervey
Hope, Arkansas 71801
(870) 777-4455

Clinton Presidential Center
1200 President Clinton Avenue
Little Rock, Arkansas 72201
(501) 374-3047

Hot Springs "Clinton Loop"
Hot Springs Convention &
    Visitors Bureau
134 Convention Boulevard
Hot Springs, Arkansas 71902
(800) 543-2284

The National First Ladies' Library
Education and Research Center
205 Market Avenue South
Canton, Ohio 44702
(330) 452-0876

United States Capitol
Constitution Avenue
Washington, D.C. 20515
(202) 225-6827

White House
1600 Pennsylvania Avenue, N.W.
Washington, D.C. 20500
(202) 456-7041

Web Sites

Clinton Presidential Center
www.clintonpresidentialcenter.org

Internet Public Library, Presidents
of the United States (IPL POTUS)
www.ipl.org/div/potus/wjclinton.html

The National Archives Clinton
Presidential Materials Project
www.clinton.archives.gov

The National First Ladies' Library
www.firstladies.org

Senator Hillary Rodham Clinton
Web site
www.clinton.senate.gov

The White House
www.whitehouse.gov

INDEX

Page numbers in **bold** represent photographs.

About the Author

Ruth Ashby has written many award-winning biographies and nonfiction books for children, including *Herstory, The Elizabethan Age,* and *Pteranodon: The Life Story of a Pterosaur.* She lives on Long Island with her husband, daughter, and dog, Nubby.